Music for S

BOOK TWO

9 Elementary Piano Duets with Student Appeal

Margaret Goldston

FOREWORD

These nine piano duets in various styles were lovingly composed for first-year students of all ages. The duets include these features, which are difficult to find in easy duet literature:

1. Both Primo and Secondo parts are at the mid-elementary level and are equivalent in difficulty to a second-level piano method book. Both parts remain in the C, G, middle-C or D position. There are usually only one or two (sometimes three or four) notes played together. Pairs of eighth notes are introduced in four of the duets. Some non-legato pedaling is indicated but is optional.

2. Some of the Primo or Secondo parts also make attractive solo pieces [see titles marked with an asterisk(s)]. As solos, they should be played as written instead of an octave higher or lower.

3. The right hand stays in the treble clef and the left hand in the bass clef to simplify the student's first experiences in sight-reading duets.

4. Students have the added pleasure of playing entertaining musical games! In "Dream" the Primo and Secondo performers can have fun taking turns playing the melody or imitating each other in measures 5–6, 9–10, 21–28, etc. as well as in the introduction and coda (measures 1–4 and 29–33). In "Let's Rock!" and "Tambourine" the Primo melody in the A section is imitated in the Secondo part of the B section.

It is my wish that when students share practice hours, weekly lessons or recital performances, they will enjoy memorable musical moments together with parents or grandparents, brothers or sisters and neighbors or friends!

CONTENTS

*The primo part may be played as a solo piece (see number 2 in Foreword).

**The primo and secondo parts may each be played as a solo piece (see number 2 in Foreword).

Art direction: Ted Engelbart   Cover design: Trish Meyer   Music engraving: Nancy Butler

Happy-Go-Lucky

SECONDO

Margaret Goldston

Brightly

(Both hands one octave lower than written throughout)

Happy-Go-Lucky

PRIMO

Brightly

(Both hands one octave higher than written throughout)

Margaret Goldston

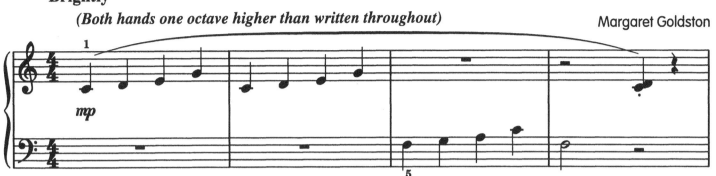

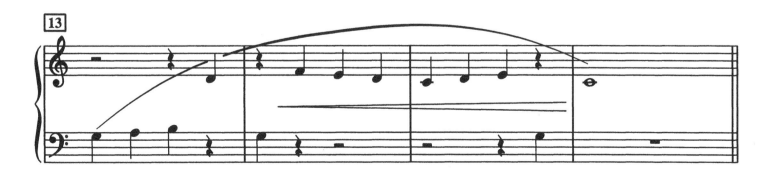

4

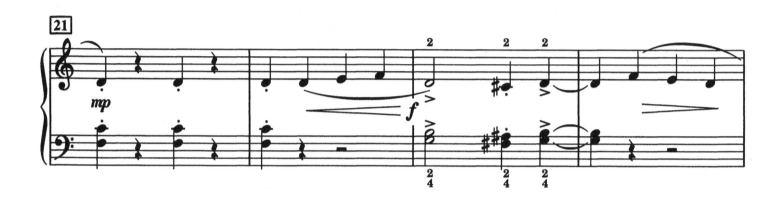

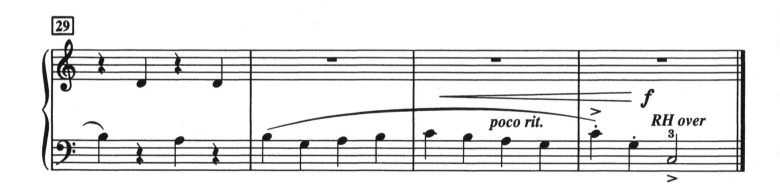

PRIMO

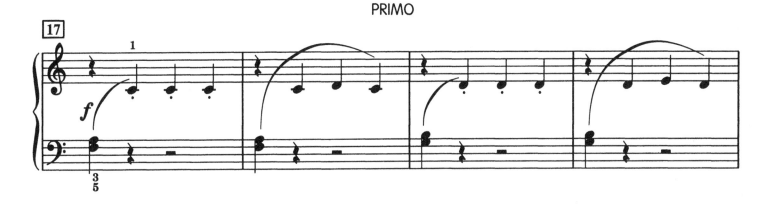

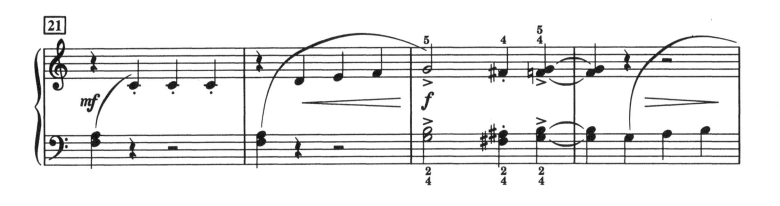

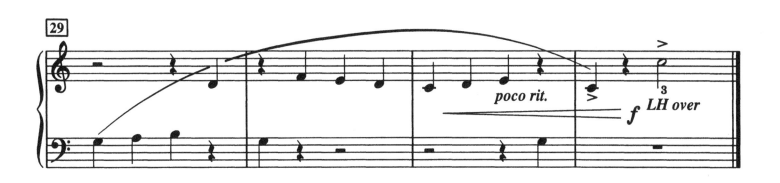

Music Box

SECONDO

Tenderly

(Both hands as written throughout)

Margaret Goldston

una corda pedal the second time

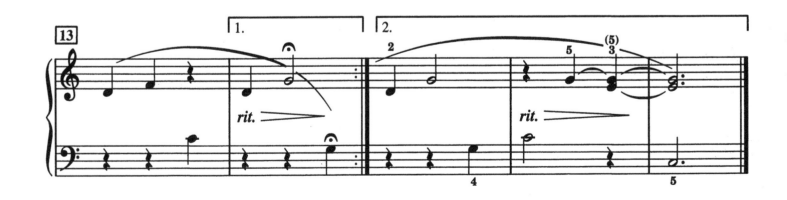

Music Box

PRIMO

Tenderly

*(Both hands two octaves higher than written the 1st time;
three octaves higher than written the 2nd time)*

Margaret Goldston

1. *(3 octaves higher than written on repeat)*

2. *(Continue 3 octaves higher to the end)*

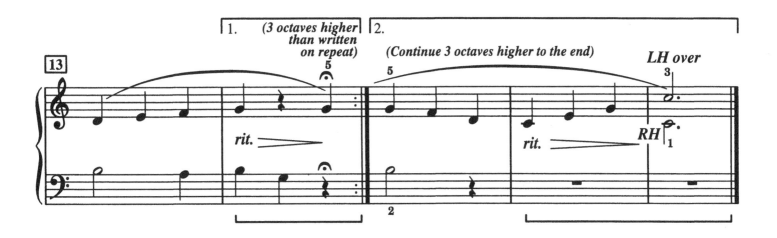

Tambourine

SECONDO

Margaret Goldston

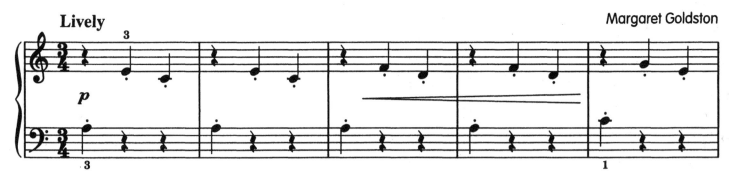

(Both hands one octave lower than written throughout)

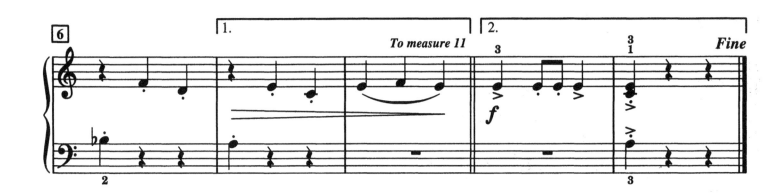

Tambourine

PRIMO

Lively

(Both hands one octave higher than written throughout)

Margaret Goldston

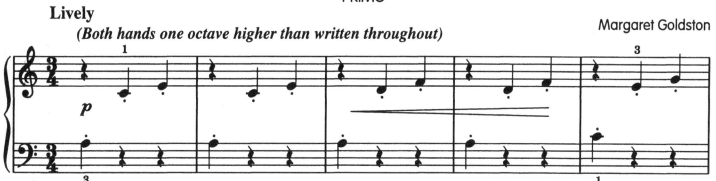

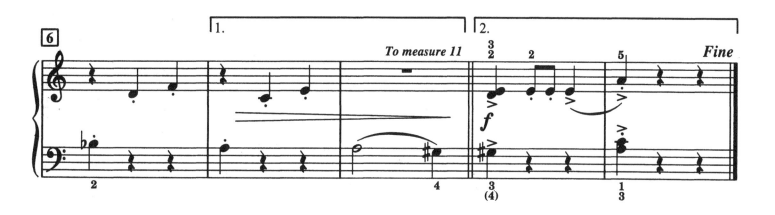

SECONDO

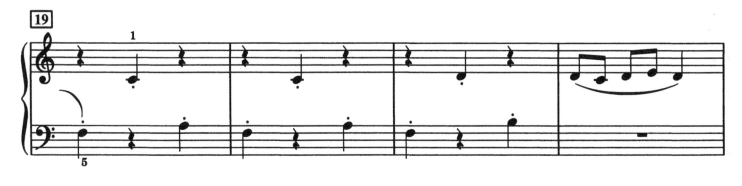

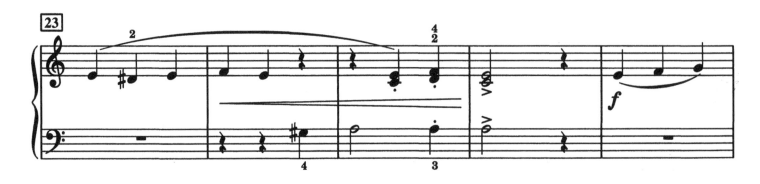

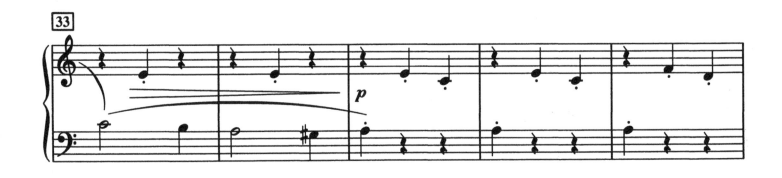

D. C. al Fine

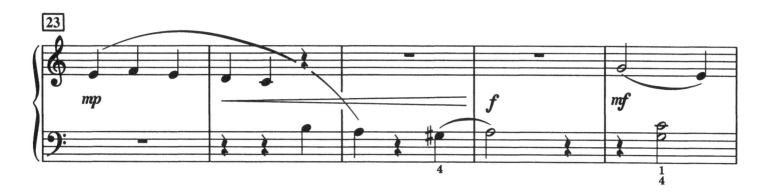

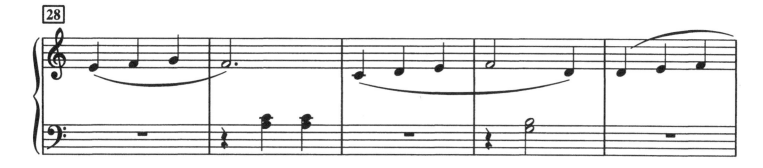

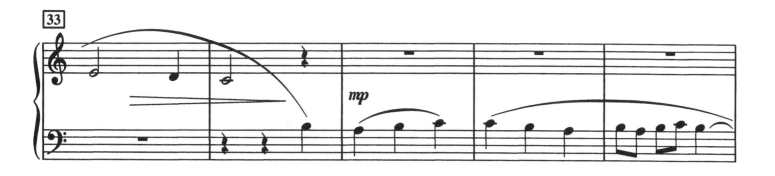

D. C. al Fine

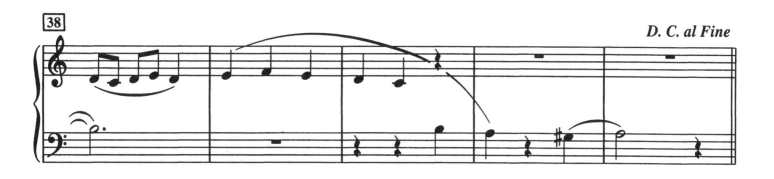

Magical March

SECONDO

With precision

Margaret Goldston

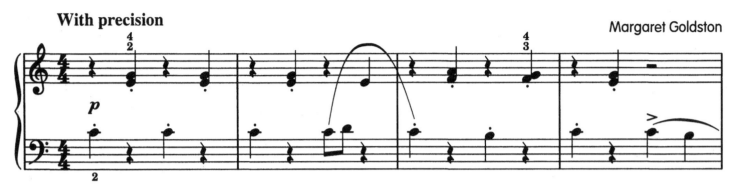

(Both hands one octave lower than written throughout)

Magical March

PRIMO

With precision

(Both hands one octave higher than written throughout)

Margaret Goldston

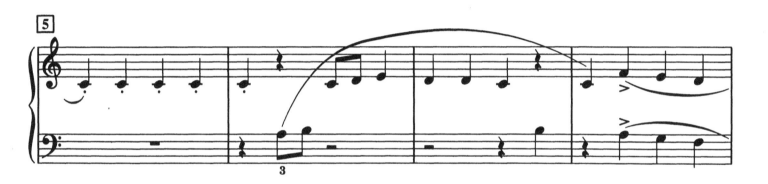

SECONDO

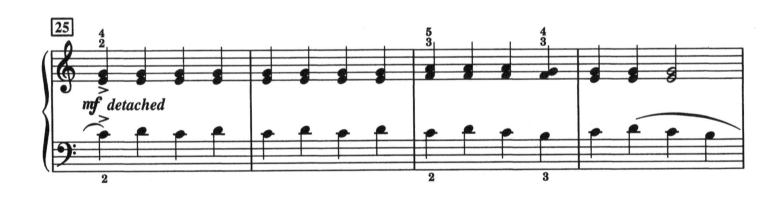

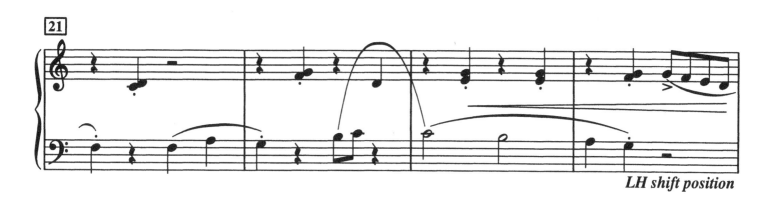

LH shift position

LH over

Autumn Mist

SECONDO

Delicately drifting

(RH one octave lower than written throughout)

Margaret Goldston

(LH as written)

una corda pedal throughout

mf

poco rit.

Autumn Mist

PRIMO

Delicately drifting

(Both hands one octave higher than written throughout)

Margaret Goldston

Ped. opt.

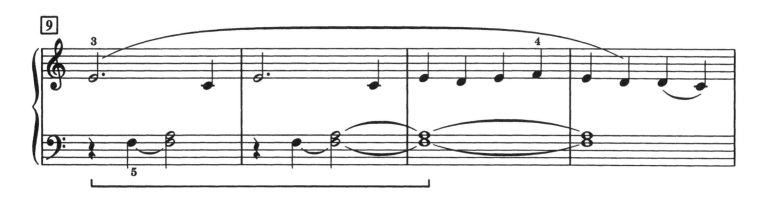

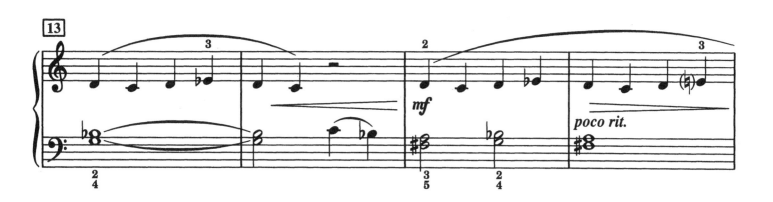

poco rit.

SECONDO

PRIMO

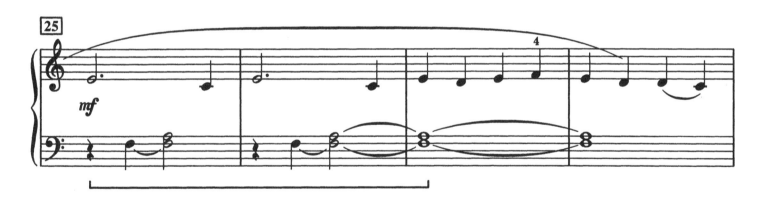

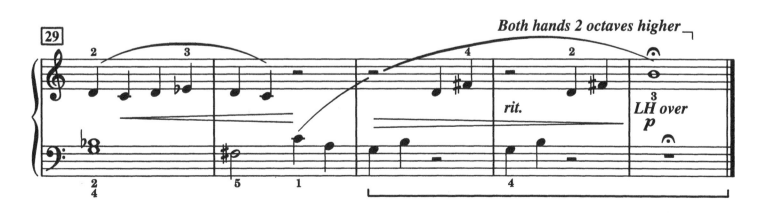

Let's Rock!

SECONDO

Margaret Goldston

With a beat

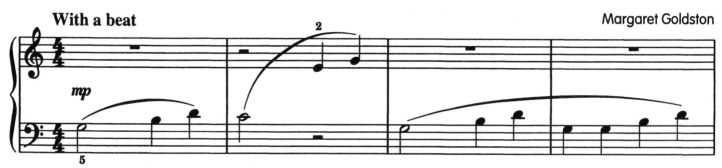

(Both hands one octave lower than written throughout)

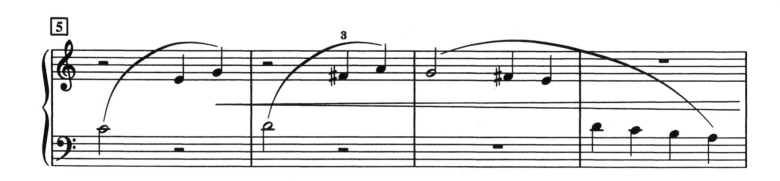

Let's Rock!

PRIMO

With a beat

(Both hands one octave higher than written throughout)

Margaret Goldston

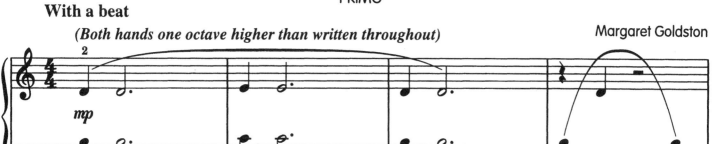

SECONDO

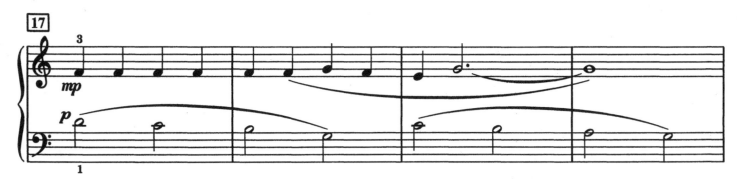

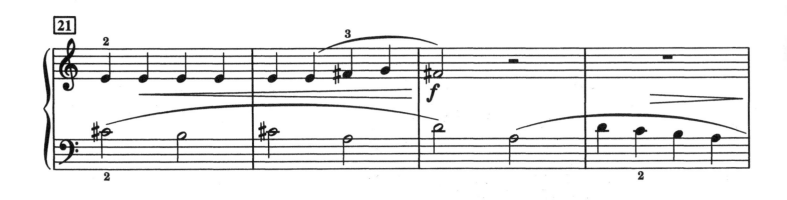

*When played as a solo, the last chord should be played:

PRIMO

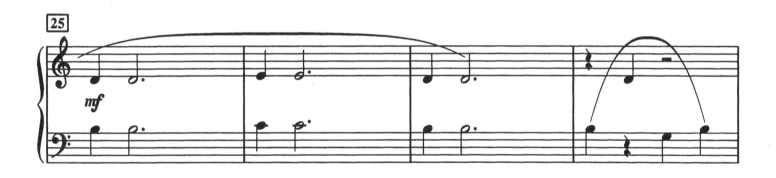

Dream

SECONDO

Peacefully, smoothly

(Both hands as written throughout)

Margaret Goldston

una corda pedal throughout

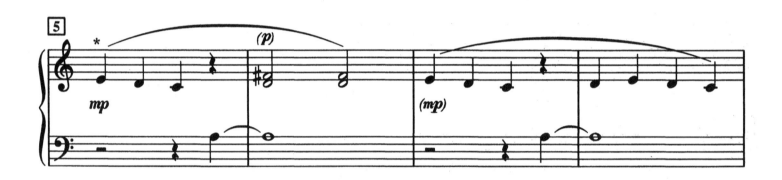

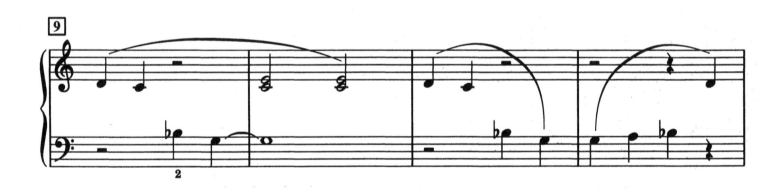

*The quarter note melody should be played louder than the half note chordal accompaniment.

Dream

PRIMO

Peacefully, smoothly

Margaret Goldston

(Both hands two octaves higher than written throughout)

Ped. opt.

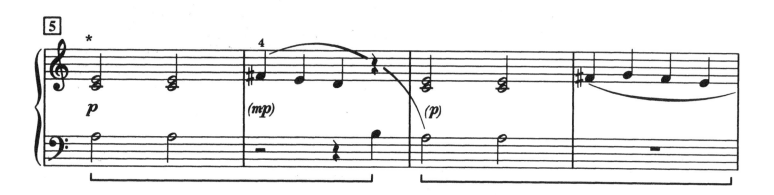

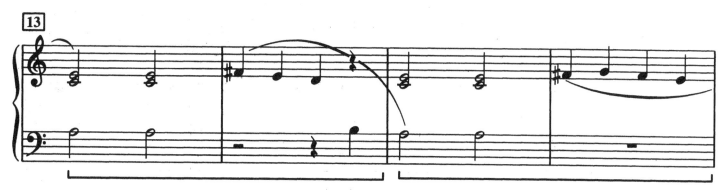

*The quarter note melody should be played louder than the half note chordal accompaniment.

SECONDO

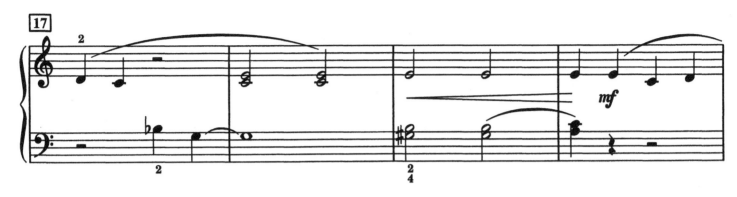

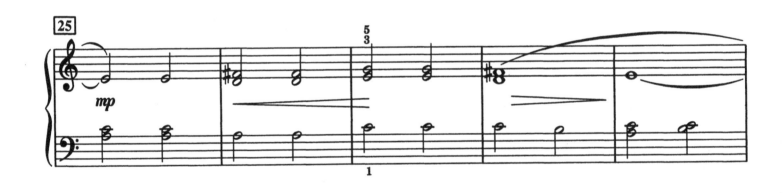

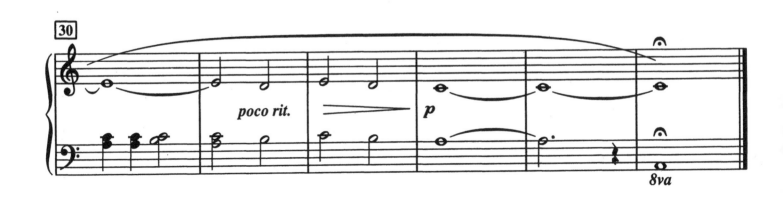

8va

PRIMO

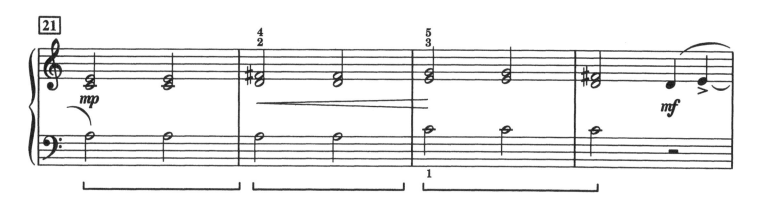

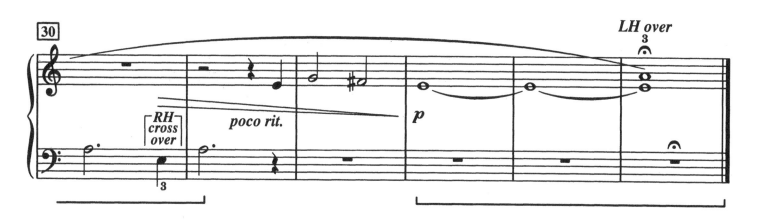

For Gayle Kowalchyk and E.L. Lancaster

Hula Dancer

SECONDO

Gently swaying
(RH one octave lower than written throughout)

Margaret Goldston

Ped. opt.

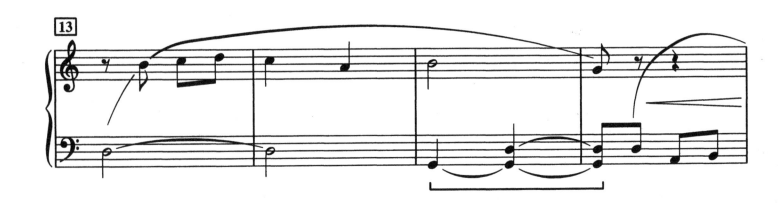

For Gayle Kowalchyk and E.L. Lancaster

Hula Dancer

PRIMO

Gently swaying

(Both hands one octave higher than written throughout)

Margaret Goldston

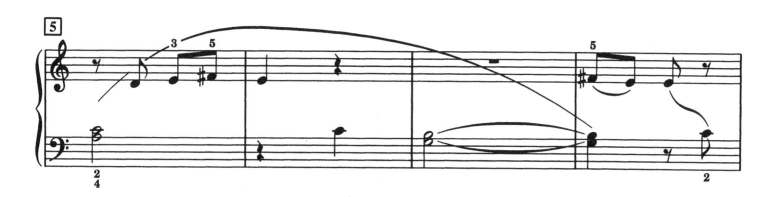

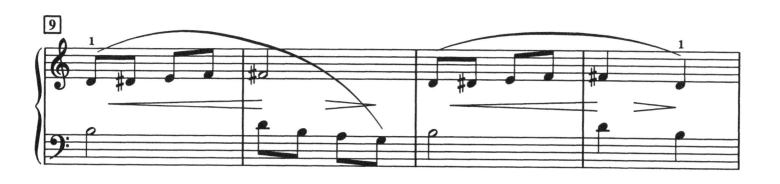

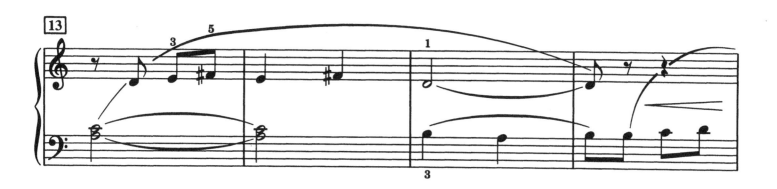

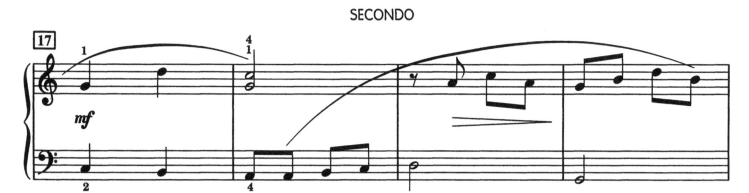

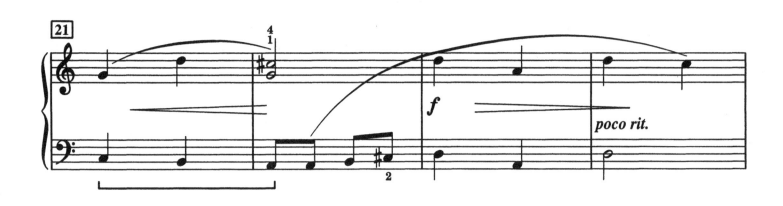

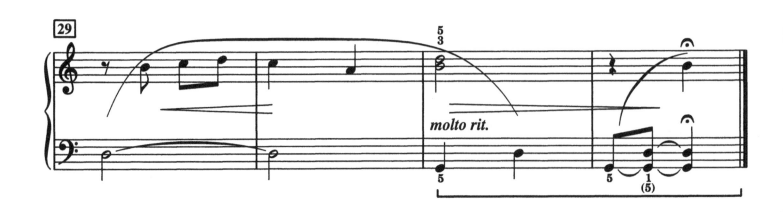

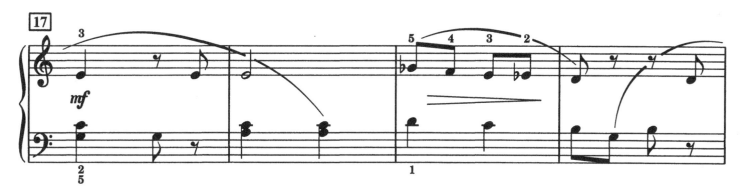

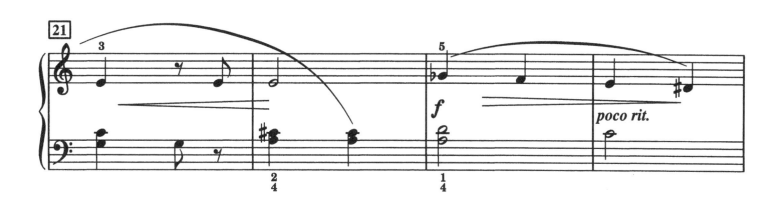

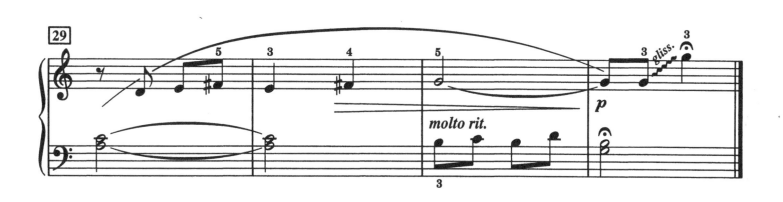

Fanfare

PRIMO

With spirit

(Both hands one octave higher than written throughout)

Margaret Goldston

Ped. opt.

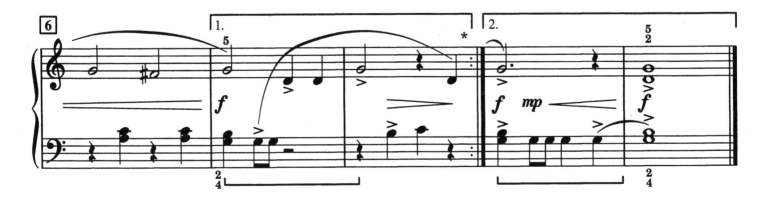

Fanfare

SECONDO

With spirit

(Both hands one octave lower than written throughout)

Margaret Goldston

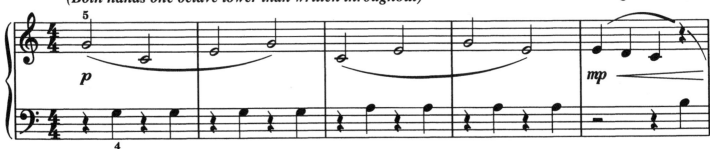

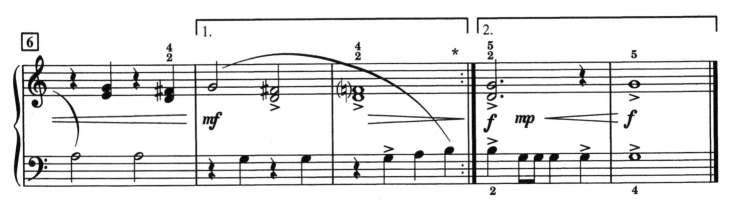

*This duet may be used as an introduction to "Magical March", "Happy-Go-Lucky", or any other lively C Major duet. When used as an introduction, the performers should continue on to the second duet immediately after the first ending of "Fanfare."